T0063512

Don't Be in the Dog House with God

A Step-by-Step Guide to Bible History

Jere` Ratcliffe Burgins-Mitchell

WestBow
PRESS
A DIVISION OF THOMAS NELSON

Scriptures taken from the Holy Bible, New International Version®, NIV®. Copyright © 1973, 1978, 1984, 2011 by Biblica, Inc.™ Used by permission of Zondervan. All rights reserved worldwide. www.zondervan.com The "NIV" and "New International Version" are trademarks registered in the United States Patent and Trademark Office by Biblica, Inc.™

Scripture taken from the New King James Version. Copyright 1979, 1980, 1982 by Thomas Nelson, inc. Used by permission. All rights reserved.

WestBow Press books may be ordered through booksellers or by contacting:

WestBow Press
A Division of Thomas Nelson
1663 Liberty Drive
Bloomington, IN 47403
www.westbowpress.com
1 (866) 928-1240

Because of the dynamic nature of the Internet, any web addresses or links contained in this book may have changed since publication and may no longer be valid. The views expressed in this work are solely those of the author and do not necessarily reflect the views of the publisher, and the publisher hereby disclaims any responsibility for them.

Any people depicted in stock imagery provided by Thinkstock are models, and such images are being used for illustrative purposes only.
Certain stock imagery © Thinkstock.

ISBN: 978-1-4908-0964-9 (sc)
ISBN: 978-1-4908-0965-6 (e)

Library of Congress Control Number: 2013917387

Printed in the United States of America.

WestBow Press rev. date: 09/30/2013

Table of Contents

Introduction vii
Dedication to my Sons ix
        And Warning to Young Women and Young
        Mothers to Be ix
        Young Women and Young Mothers to Be.......................x

Chapter 1   Don't Be In the Dog House with God 1
        Step-By-Step Guide to Bible History 1
Chapter 2   A Fuller Understanding 5
        A Detail Rapture of the Biblical Times........................5
Chapter 3   Let's Examine 10
        Bible History Therapy 10
Chapter 4   New Testament Beginning...16
        Climb Into Comfy Bible History 16
Chapter 5   New Testament Beginning Continued.......................22
        Moses...22
Chapter 6   New Testament Beginning continues..........................26
        The mosaic Age...26
Chapter 7   The Judges and the Kings...35
Chapter 8   The Prophets 42
Chapter 9   A Magnificent Man 45
Chapter 10 The Purpose 50

The Christian Now!...50

Chapter 11 Examining the Kingdom 58

Chapter 12 The Early Christians......................................63

Conclusion 63

In Closing 64

My Prayer...65

God's Part: God's Plan of Salvation............................66

Man's Part: Obedience 66

Introduction

Preaching is the most unique way of reaching spiritual minded people who wishes to serve God in hopes to have eternal life someday with Him. It is a reflection of God's Mind when Ministers teach us how to live God's way.

For me, as a Bible student, and as is my duty, the author and a dedicated servant of our Lord and Savior, I want to reach people with every day simple language. In other words simplify the Word of God for those who need simplification to get the knowledge they need and the full understanding of what will save their souls.

This is not in any way fringing on the theological book and the preacher's teachings, but a book for those of us who have difficulty in understanding some terms and issues set forth in the Bible that confuses man. It is an introduction to some basic wisdom and truths of what we should know in order to fully understand the Bible's whys do and do not as well as understand why we are here in the first place.

Don't Be In The Dog House With God! Points out the challenges the people before us encountered that have provided insight for our lives today. Even in the struggles of hard times it tells us what is expected of us and how we should live and at the same time, we have the choice of what we want to believe and obey.

Don't Be In The Dog House With God! has substance but not difficult to read. I recommend it to everyone who cares about his/her being.

Dedication to my Sons

AND WARNING TO YOUNG WOMEN AND YOUNG MOTHERS TO BE

To my three sons, one is deceased, Charles Edward Burgins Jr. His death was due to a malignant inoperable brain tumor, treated at Stanford Hospital, in Palo Alto, California. The two sons remaining are Ray David Burgins and Robert Ronald Burgins. I and my three sons was a foursome as they grew up into adulthood and they are a joy to me.

With the Airman Husband no longer in our lives, left me to be a young mother who had no idea of the needs of male children, and I specify male children. I felt keeping a roof over their heads, food in their mouths and clothes on their backs would be sufficient. I was not aware that men children should be taught how to be responsible or even to have religious values that I thought as with me came naturally or teach them how to save money and the entire lessons that creates maturity. The results are extraordinary men who basically matured on their own.

In this Dedication, I humbly thank my sons for being my sons and I apologize for my ignorance.

Young Women and Young Mothers to Be

For your own peace of mind for years to come, don't grow up too! Fast without investigating the consequences.

Don't be like me being an unsuccessful young bride who ends up rearing children alone. Believe me having babies because you feel it's no big deal is one of the biggest mistakes in your life that you can make.

It's a jungle out there and you need to make it right and understandable for any off-spring you should happen to bring into this world. Being careful of every Tom, Dick and Harry you meet and which one is worth your time and mean you well.

Be careful who you bed down with because the Bible has already given us an example to bed with whom, why and when. Allow me to explain further in the upcoming book called Women, Women, Women God said . . . !

Chapter I

Don't Be In the Dog House with God

STEP-BY-STEP GUIDE TO BIBLE HISTORY

Let's Talk
Life Itself is Bible History

When I say "Picture this," remember now, I am speaking from a human perspective, because this next section is not scriptural but, none-the-less, let's Picture this! Let's say, every human being now living on earth once lived as a spirit in the Spirit World called Heaven. This is something to really think about.

Say we are the same spirits then as we are now. And in this fantasy Spirit World called Heaven trouble began with Satan wanting to be God, yet being a leader full of defiance and ugliness. And as it has always been, whether in fantasy land or since the world began, some of the spirits became his followers. This I believe is similar to the discord in the real Heaven when Satan was casted out of it?

Welcome to my home.

I am offering you to sit in my over-stuffed chair, I think you will be quite comfortable there and I am so glad you came by because there are a few things I'd like to hash over with you.

One thing that is on my mind is when I hear and I know you also have heard people say, "I hope to see you in Heaven or I will see you in Heaven."

Well my thoughts on that are, to recognize one's spirit, how could it be if we had not known one another before in Heaven as a spirit? That is why I came up with the 'Picture This Fantasy. People are always saying little clichés that they don't stop to think about what they are saying.

With that question asked or the fantasy speculation, we know it is only human thinking and human logic. And to tell you the truth, it's really none of our business but to do God's Will in hopes we can spend eternity with Him, because our thoughts and our ways are not God's thoughts and ways according to many scriptures in the Bible and here is one that emphasizes that very thought, Isaiah 55:9. Here God lets us know, "For as the Heavens are higher than the earth, so are My ways higher than your ways, and My thoughts than your thoughts." So, therefore, no one have any idea who, when where and how a human will see anyone anywhere after death.

So, we ought to be careful how we interpret the Bible don't you think? After all it is God's Words speaking to us and He does not need our interpretation or help.

God the Father being all knowing, all seeing, all giving, all planning, casting Satan out of Heaven, God a merciful God, created the earth and God allowed Satan to be king over all those who wish to continue following him, while God's only begotten Son Jesus Christ would come to earth and become the Redeemer and the Savior with the promise of eternal life for those who will accept, believe, trust and follow Him the Lord and Savior, Jesus Christ.

Let's stop here for a moment and talk about Satan . . . Yeah Satan!

I've always heard that Satan was casted out of Heaven but, some people say he fell out of Heaven, so I decided the best thing for me to do is to go searching for the truth.

Satan fell spiritually before he tempted Adam and Eve in the Garden Genesis 3:1-14. Yet, the book of Job tells us that Satan still could go to Heaven and to the throne of God to talk with God.

One day angels came before the LORD, and Satan also came with them. The Lord said to Satan, 'Where have you come from?' Satan answered the Lord, "From roaming throughout the earth, going back and forth on it." (Job 1:7)

Why did Satan fall from Heaven? Satan fell because of pride. "I will . . ." was all he knew to say in Isaiah 14:12-15 Satan desired to be God" and wanted to take over the rule of life.

So did Satan fall from heaven? No! A fall is not what happened. It would be more accurate to say God cast Satan out of Heaven according to Isaiah 14:12-15. More bluntly put, Satan did not fall from Heaven; Satan was pushed out of heaven. Therefore, we must believe, love and follow Jesus.

Honestly now, without the hope of eternal life, what else is there?

Everyone human living has the free-well to choose what king they which to serve, either Satan or Jesus. We can't have it both ways. As in Ephesians Chapter six and verse twelve tells us that we are not fighting with each other that are made of flesh and blood but against persons without bodies, in other words as the King James Version puts it, "For we wrestle not against flesh and blood but against principalities, against Spiritual wickedness in high places."

If you will remember in the beginning of my story I said, "Picture this" Now the Bible, God's Word doesn't tell my story in the fantasy style I gave, but in the verse I just quoted to you is a fact. God certainly did give us the privilege to make choices, and it is evident that we can't have two masters; we either love one or hate the other. There is no two ways about it. No straddling the fence. This is God's requirement, not mine.

A quote from our first President, George Washington said, "It is impossible to rightly govern the world without God and the Bible," and I agree.

Let's began talking. I guarantee you that the remainder of 'Don't Be in the Dog House with God!' is facts connecting Old Bible times with our time.

What kind of Hostess am I! Here allow me to pour you a cup of tea while we breakdown how the Bible is constructed.

The Breakdown

Old Testament: Pentateuch (Books of Law), also called Patriarchal Time (meaning Male Controlled), next is Books of Poetry, Minor Prophets.

Then (400 silent years)
New Testament
History-Gospels
Church History
General Letters
Revelation—Prophecies

But to date, there is just one time in history that God Himself treasures and endorses and who He has given on this earth all Authority is His only begotten Son, Jesus Christ.

For us to really know God's Will and to get the big picture, I must begin at the Beginning of His Bible's History.

Chapter II

A Fuller Understanding

A DETAIL RAPTURE OF THE BIBLICAL TIMES

During the first period of Bible History, God ruled men through the heads of families, called the Pentateuch. The Pentateuch consisted of the first 5 books of the Old Testament. The word Pentateuch (pehn' tuh teuhch) comes from two Greek words Penta "five" and teuchos meaning "box," "jar," or "scroll."

The Bible begins with Genesis. It consists of the creation, the fall, the Flood, and the spread of the nations which are Abraham, Isaac, Jacob, Joseph and the enslavement in Egypt.

In Exodus, the enslavement continued. Then came Moses, and the ten plagues, the Passover, the children of Israel Leaving Egypt, the Red Sea Crossing, on Mt. Sinai where the Ten Commandments given to them by the finger of God.

The Leviticus gives Instructions on the sacrificial system and the priesthood. Also it gives instructions on how to be clothed decently.

Numbers tells us that while Moses was still on Mt. Sinai, the people made false idols and their punishment was the beginning of forty years wandering in the wilderness.

Deuteronomy is when Moses' addresses God's activities for Israel and the ceremonials begin, civil and social Laws introduced, and the covenant confirmed.

As you see, from the beginning of creation, this Pentateuch time, also known as the Biblical times, reaches all the way to the time of Moses and the exit of God's people in the land of Egypt.

Following the Pentateuch Books is the 12 Historical Books. In Joshua, the first half of Joshua describes the 7-year defeat of the Land of Promise. And the last half deals with dividing the lands to the people.

Judges tells us that this was a bad period in time. The Israelites did not drive out all the citizens of Canaan and therefore they began to take part in the Canaanite's Idol worship and consequently, the Israelites didn't learn anything from their hardships.

Ruth, a Moabite, communicates righteousness, love and faithfulness to the Lord and introduces Boaz as the rescuer in saving Ruth.

Now the next 6 books trace the time from Samuel to the Captivity.

In First Samuel, Samuel carries Israel from judges to King Saul.

Second Samuel is about David being King, commits adultery, and murder.

First Kings, shows that with King Solomon as King, Israel is powerful. Then Solomon dies. After Solomon's death, the tribes were divided into twelve tribes. Ten tribes went to the north and two tribes to the south.

Second Kings shows the history of the Divided Kingdom. All nineteen kings of Israel were bad; therefore, they were in captivity in Assyria (722 B.C.). In Judah, eight of twenty rulers were good but they went into exile also.

First Chronicles describes the history of Israel to the time of Solomon.

And Second Chronicles continues the describing of the life of Solomon, the building of the temple, to the captivity. It's the History of Judah only.

The Next 3 books deal with Israel's Restoration.

Ezra is where Cyrus let most of the Jews return to their land, Israel. Zerubbabel led the people in 539 B.C. Then, Ezra returned later with more Jews in 458 B.C. and built the temple.

Nehemiah built the walls of Jerusalem. Nehemiah got permission from the king of Persia to rebuild the walls in 444 B.C. and there was strengthening in that land.

Esther took place during chapters six and seven of Ezra. There was Mordecai, and also a Plot to kill the Jewish people.

Following Ester is the five Poetical Books: Beginning with Job, who was a righteous man and who was tested by God.

Psalms consists of five divisions. Worship in song and a large variety of subjects.

Proverbs expresses practical wisdom in everyday concerns.

Ecclesiastes shows that all is vanity and the wisdom of man is worthless.

Song of Solomon is a song between Solomon and his Shulammite bride, displaying the love between a man and a woman.

When summing the Books up, there are seventeen Prophetical Books, five Books of the Major Prophets, and twelve Books of the Minor Prophets.

Then there were 400 silent years between Malachi, the last book of the Old Testament to the first Book Mathew, in the New Testament.

Now in this lifetime, we do not have God talking directly to us as He did in the Old History Biblical times where certain sins caused a person to be stoned to death. But! We do have the Bible as God's means of communicating with us, giving us His guidelines how He wishes us to live. Thank God for that. Yes! Indeed.

Of course you may say, "But it was written by human men. And I'd say, "Yes, it was written by men, but by men whom God chose and inspired—and no human man can prove differently." The Bible is the only Book that reveals where man came from and all of us will be judged by this Bible, living or dead. After all, this Book, called the Bible tells the purpose of our being here on earth in the first place and what to believe, who to serve, how to live and what to do daily to live someday with God Himself eternally. Living with God is my hope of accomplishment and I hope it is yours too!

Now concerning these men who wrote the Bible, there were about forty of them from differing backgrounds and cultures. They wrote the Bible over a period of 1500 years and these writers were guided by Divine Wisdom. So you see the Bible is the Mind of God. It is written for us humans to understand what His Will is for us to do and how He wants us to do it. He is in control and He is the Creator. Surely you have read that the apostle Peter said, "For the prophecy came not in the old time by the will of men, but Holy men of God spoke as they were moved by the Holy Spirit" (2 Peter 1:21).

Even in the days of Noah, God let Noah and His family know that the people had become wicked and that He was sorry He had created man so therefore, He was going to destroy the earth with all the people on it and since Noah was a righteous man he and his family would be safe providing he follow God's directions.

So who are we, because the same applies to us today? Obedience to God's Will is the key. It is necessary and the most important thing we must do in life.

Now let me explain these Books of the Bible further for our learning and understanding more clearly and for our development.

As we talked about earlier, there are three periods in our history with God. And they are the Pentateuch Age, the Mosaic Age, and the Christian Age. We learned that In the Pentateuch Age, God spoke to the head of the households like Adam. The second period God gave Moses His law but in the third period, He gave us the Gospel that came by Jesus Christ.

For example: After Jesus Christ was crucified and according to the Book of Acts, Things changed.

Now, in this time, when a person desires to be a Christian is certainly different than the Pentateuch Age and the Mosaic age.

For us now, we do not slaughter goats and make sacrificial offerings because Jesus Christ is our sacrificial Lamb.

Knowing about the three periods you can more intelligently understand the Bible and God's Will and plans for us today. It also shows us how to study the Bible and apply it more wisely and appreciate it. Keep in mind as we study and learn more of God's Ways and Wills that He created everything that we know and enjoy on this earth,

Heaven and everything living, from the smallest bug to the colossal beast. Further, He made man from dust of the earth and breathed into him the breath of life and man became a living soul. A far cry from man's idea of humans coming from monkeys as has been said or any other far-fetched idea that humans' imagination out grows itself.

And after all of God's work, and keep in mind, not man's work or monkeys' work, on the seventh day He saw that all He had done was good so, He blessed the seventh day and made it holy, because on that day He needed to rest.

Chapter III

Let's Examine

BIBLE HISTORY THERAPY

The Bible is fascinating as it reveals its truths and history, which prepares us for eternity. At first the earth was a shapeless mass of nothing. It had no form. It was void of people, fish and whatever, you name it. It just didn't exist. And to top it all off, it was dark; pitch black . . . can't see your hand before your face. Then suddenly! A Voice, God's Voice says, "Let there be light!" And there was light. He made the greater light to rule the day and the lesser light to rule the night as we know the two lights. These two great lights that we take for granted and enjoy so much. God indeed spoke the Words and the greater light and the lesser light then existed.

After the Creation, Adam, a man who was formed from dirt and who being dear to God was given the honor in naming the animals. Then God saw after all He gave Adam to have control of, still Adam was unhappy, he was lonely.

We know how loneliness feels. Can't you imagine being on a desert Island all alone just looking at the beauty around you? The chirping of the birds, the sea creatures mating, the alligators resting, the monkeys jumping from limb to limb and the fish smooching, yet you are so all alone?

God saw the human loneliness and had sympathy for Adam, so God caused Adam to fall into a deep sleep; and while he was sleeping, He took one of Adam's ribs and after removing the one rib and closing the incision with Adam's flesh the Lord God made a woman from the rib. He brought her to Adam. This was the first marriage and cure for loneliness.

After God showed His mercifulness, all of His goodness and kindness, the first sin was committed. Now on earth there was no longer innocence. The first lie and the first murder were committed. And the earth became populated. In time, it became filled with wickedness. So this wickedness caused God to be filled with disappointment, so much so that His Will was obeyed to destroy what He had created in that Great Flood we can read about with only eight righteous souls saved from it.

As God restocked the earth with people, Abraham, Isaac, Jacob and Joseph were the next characters to focus on. And then there's the intriguing story of Joseph in Egypt. Even later on, how God freed Israel through Moses.

When God placed Adam and Eve in a wonderland on earth, He also allowed them to make choices and we are allowed the same privilege.

God placed Adam and Eve among the breathtaking, sweet smelling flowers cascading green vines, amazing bushes and magnificent trees in the garden. Two trees of importance stood out among the trees in the Garden of Eden—the Tree of the Knowledge of Good and Evil and the Tree of Life. God chose one of those two trees and specified that Adam and Eve were not to eat of it and that was the tree of good and evil. That particular tree is also known as one knowing good and bad and better yet, knowing right from wrong. It was clear that God told them personally, "Do not eat of that tree!" And as it has been proven, humans are just obviously bold and self-willed. Even with that stern warning, they disobeyed any way and attempted to place blame. But look what happened, when they disobeyed God and ate of the forbidden tree, they created the first sin and that is the only thing humans created. So therefore, this human creation causes us to be born into sin? Not born sinful but born into sin. As we grow, we indulge in sin more willfully and as we grow we still have the choice of knowing the difference of right from wrong and are capable of choosing which one we wish to follow.

When Adam and Eve choose to be disobedient to God, it caused a separation from Him. That is what sin is, a sad separation from God. That separation from God means what it means, when we are disobedient to God, we will suffer the consequences.

Adam and Eve did a first class act for us, I'd say.

You see as I repeat, God had given them the ability to make choices. In other words let their minds think righteously and be obedient to His Will, yet still are independent in choosing to do right in God's eye sight.

God had clearly warned Adam and Eve that if they disobeyed what He had commanded of them, they would surely die. The word death or die was not like the death as we know death; it means as stated before, "separation" from God. Just as when we won't be obedient to what we know is God's Words in His Bible, where there it explains His Will is to be done by us, whether we like it or not or whether we choose to believe it or not, the fact remains, we are being disobedient when we give a deaf ear and ignore them, then we are separated from God. I don't believe this can be stressed enough.

You must understand, separation from God means spiritual death and eternal Grief.

With Adam and Eve thrown out of the garden of paradise and away from the eternal tree of life, we are born to die and we have the choice of spiritually dying as well.

Aside from the mess Adam and Eve has placed us in; our merciful Father in Heaven still gives us hope because Jesus proved to us that we could overcome this spiritual death through Him.

This is how it works.

You see first God gave Adam a warning telling him that "You may eat of any tree in the garden except from the Tree of Knowledge for its fruit will open your eyes to make you aware of right and wrong, good and bad and if you eat of this tree Adam," God continued, "you will surely die." And Adam passed these words on to his wife, Eve. So now both of them were aware of God's Will and warning. Now having been disobedient their eyes were opened to the good and the bad, they could see the differences in their bodies and knowing that their bodies were exposed for all to see, including God. This is something they weren't aware of before when they weren't disobedient. But, wouldn't you know, God still showed compassion on them.

First because He knew they were embarrassed of their new awareness so He dressed their naked bodies with garments made from the skins of animals. None-the-less, since Adam and Eve willingly was disobedient to God's warning; it caused all mankind to be doomed forever.

Second, God again shows compassion for humans by providing sacrificial animals to sacrifice for their sins. You must realize this animal sacrifice was temporary because His greater Sacrifice He knew would be perfect and later is offered to us for payment in full for our sins.

Adam had no choice but to toil for his living now and Eve had to bare pain in childbearing. Then the Lord said to the serpent, (the one who enticed Eve), "This is your punishment: You are singled out from among all the domestic and wild animals of the whole earth to be cursed. You shall crawl on your belly in the dust as long as you live."

So now, the couple knew that they had no other option but to obey God's command and that was to "multiply and fill up the earth with their off springs. The first two children of theirs were Cain and Abel. And as time went by, Cain was a farmer and was uncaring in his worship to God, and gave little concern what he offered God for sacrifice from the blessings God blessed him with for his labor. Cain gave God as some people give others today, what they have no use for and no longer want.

On the other hand, Abel, the younger of Adam and Eve's sons was a shepherd and by his faith in believing in God for who God is and how he respected Him, he gave the very best of his lambs to God for his spiritual sacrifice of thankfulness for the love and mercy God had shown him.

God was pleased with Abel and I am sure you can feel the smile that was possibly on God's face for having such a devoted loving person such as Abel as we should hope to put a twinkle in God's eyes too!

But from Cain, He was not pleased. Can't you imagine how God must have felt to see how ungrateful Cain was in his heart for the corps God allowed him to harvest? How thoughtless, selfish and full of vanity he was and that his wisdom was worthless. And there are many humans like that today.

That is like some of us today with the Big "I" I this and I that, not giving one iota where their fortunes come from, be it health wise or material wealth. Not seeing that the all mighty Heavenly Father taking care of His beloved children.

A good example found in Ecclesiastes concerning Self-Indulgence in chapter 2, it reads: I undertook great projects: I built houses for myself and planted vineyards. I made gardens and parks and planted all kinds of fruit trees in them. I made reservoirs to water groves of flourishing trees. I bought male and female slaves and had other slaves who were born in my house. I also owned more herds and flocks than anyone in Jerusalem before me. I collected silver and gold for myself, and the treasure of kings and provinces. I acquired male and female singers, and a harem as well—I became greater by far than anyone in Jerusalem before me.

Let's face it; there are two kinds of worships. God really does know our hearts and He knows just how willing we will love Him and how we will crave to please Him. It doesn't matter if we are like the little old lady that could only give Him a penny, and it was all she had but she gave it any way to her Lord and Master willingly. To the one she believed loved her and would take care of her. We should have like mind, whether we feel it is old fashioned or not. God's Words and Desires are always fashionable.

Don't misread what I am saying. I am not saying God does not want us to have beautiful things, after all He provides "things" for us. But, where is in our hearts when we acquire them. Do we stop to realize God is responsible for all we have? Do we give Him credit and thanks or do you think we acquired everything all by ourselves or everything just happen by chance. If the latter is how we feel, then we have not read Luke 12:15 and if we are not familiar with the Bible, here is what it says.

Then he said to them, "Watch out! Be on your guard against all kinds of greed; life does not consist in an abundance of possessions."

And in 1 John 2:15-17 spells it out even better.

"Do not love the world or anything in the world. If anyone loves the world, love for the Father is not in them. For everything in the world—the lust of the flesh, the lust of the eyes, and the pride of life—comes not from the Father but from the world. The world and its desires pass away, but whoever does the Will of God lives forever.

Need I say more?

In other words, first there are those who worship according to God's instructions and the second kind of worship is those who worship but not in keeping with God's will. And in this kind of worship it is called worshiping in vain. Actually, if we are not following God's rules, then we are doing our own thing because God's ways and Thoughts and Will are not man's thoughts and ways. Sadly man unfortunately forgets who is in control and whose Will is to be obeyed.

For My thoughts are not your thoughts, neither are your ways My ways, said the Lord . . . **God** has the right to expect and demand that every human being live according to His Will.

God will not accept man's substitutes.

God is an awesome God even when He had been disappointed and grieved painfully in His Heart, He still wanted to cleanse the earth and give humans another opportunity to be righteous and serve Him and Him alone.

You know humans are still ridiculously self-willed today as they were in the days of the Old Testament. As it was then, today people are doubters when it comes to the wonders of God.

Men today are using their own knowledge without consulting God. They fail to realize it is God who gave them their knowledge. And what's more devastating is that man now is attempting to take God out of everything and disregard God altogether.

In Noah's time the people were destroyed by water and today in our time, the New Testament time, we are told that the earth will be destroyed by fire and by now, we should know that God is not slack when it comes to His promises.

Chapter IV

New Testament Beginning

CLIMB INTO COMFY BIBLE HISTORY

Nine generations after the Flood, Abraham (in the beginning Abraham was known as Abram) and Isaac are introduced to the Bible History.

During those times painfully to say, Noah's descendants lost faith in God and all the men that descended from Noah, through the many generations living in the various nations that developed after the flood spoke one single language. The population of people grew and grew and as they went eastward, they found land in Babylon and there they soon thickly populated it too! These people began to talk about building a great city, with a temple-tower reaching to the sky. "This tower would surely bind us together," they said, "and it would keep us from scattering all over the world." But when God came down to see the city and the tower these men were making, He said, "Look! If they are able to accomplish all this when they have just begun to use their language and organizational unity, just think of what they will do later. There will be nothing that will be unachievable for them. Come, let us go down and give them different languages, in this way, they will not understand each other's words. So God scattered them all-over the earth. The city then was called Babel which means confusion because God confused them by giving them many languages.

So as a result, when the various languages were born and people were scattered all over the earth and as before, the population increased in sin.

Because of Abraham's unquestioning faith, God chose him as special and directed Abraham to leave his country with his relatives into a land where He would take them. This land would be the land where God promised through Abraham's descendants, Jesus would be born.

Repeatedly, God promised that Abraham, meaning Father of Nations where as before, his name was Abram, meaning Exalted Father, would have children as many as the sand on the seashore and as many as the stars of the sky. When God told Abraham all this, Abraham was already an old man and was getting older and childless.

Awhile later, and a few upsets, Hagar, a handmaiden of Sarai, gave birth. It was Abraham's son at the insistence of Sarai, his wife, later Sarai's name changed to Sarah, who was barren and who had given her husband to her handmaiden. After a few more painful episodes, God began to fulfill His promise to Abraham. He sent three men to Abraham in Mamre to tell Abraham that he and Sarah would have a son.

Sarai, now called Sarah, listened to what was being said between the three men and her husband when she heard the Lord say, "Next year I will give you and Sarah a son!"

Now Sarah was long since passed the time when she could have a baby. "Women my age have a baby?" She said to herself, "and with a husband as old as mine." She laughed, although she later lied and said she didn't laugh. But she did laugh.

Ah! She should have remembered as we must all remember that anything is possible with God.

Within a year, Sarah gave birth to Isaac as God promised. And Abraham named him Isaac meaning 'Laughter!'

Abraham being very old, God blessed him in every way. Not long after Abraham had buried his wife Sarah, he said to the head of his household servants who was the oldest of the servants. "Swear by Jehovah, the God of Heaven and earth, that you will not let my son marry one of these local women, these Canaanites. Go to my home land, to my relatives, and find a wife for him there." And the conversation went from the supposes and the if nots until finally, the servant vowed to follow Abraham's instructions.

So when the time came, the servant took with him ten of Abraham's camels and loaded them with samples of the best of everything his master owned, and journeyed to Iraq, to Nahor's village. He then knelt down and began to pray. "Oh Jehovah, the God of my master, show kindness to my master Abraham and help me to accomplish the purpose of my travel"

He then began trying to touch basics with God to make sure he was on the same page with Him. The Servant said, "See, here I am standing beside this spring, and the girls of the village are coming out to draw water. This is my request: When I ask one of them for a drink and she says, 'Yes, certainly and I will water your camels too!' Let her be the one you have appointed as the wife for Isaac. This is how I will know."

Before the servant had finished speaking with the Lord, a beautiful young lady named Rebecca arrived with a water jug on her shoulder and filled it at the spring.

Quickly running over to her, the servant asked her for a drink.

"Certainly, sir," she said, and lowered the jug for him to drink. Then she said, "I'll draw water for your camels, too!

The servant said no more.

This should be a lesson to us that we too can talk to our Heavenly Father in the same manner and just as our earthly father sees fit for our good and do well by us, Our Heavenly Father also for our good will answer. Talking to the Heavenly Father is just as easy as talking to our earthly father, if not easier.

In conversation, he learned that Rebecca's father was Bethuel, the son of Nahor and his wife Milcah. And immediately the servant gave thanks to the Lord for answering his prayer.

"Thank you, Lord God of my master Abraham. Thank you for being so kind and true to him and for leading me straight to the family of my master's relatives."

Rebecca ran home to tell her folks about the man she had met and when her brother Laban saw the ring, and the bracelets on his sister's wrists, and heard her story, he rushed out to the spring where the man was still standing beside his camels, and said to him, "Come and stay with us friend, why stand here outside the city when we have a room all ready for you. And a place prepared for the camels.

The servant went with Laban and he met Bethuel. He now explained the vow that he had promised to his master which was the reason for his presence before them/

Then Laban and Bethuel replied.

"The Lord has obviously brought you here, so what can we say? Take her and go! Yes, let her be the wife of your master's son, as Jehovah has directed.

They called Rebecca and asked her, "Are you willing to go with this man?"

She replied, "Yes, I will go."

So with a blessing, they told her good bye, sending along with her the woman who had been her childhood nurse.

Meanwhile, Isaac, whose home was in the Negeb, had returned to Beer-Lahtai-roi.

One evening as he was taking a walk out in the fields, meditating, he looked up and saw the camels coming and began walking toward them.

Rebecca noticed him and quickly dismounted. "Who is this man coming toward us," she inquired.

Abraham's servant replied, "It is my master's son!

So she quickly covered her face with her veil.

Isaac approached them and the servant told him the whole story.

Then Isaac brought Rebecca into his mother's tent, and she became his wife. He loved her so very much and she was a special comfort to him since the loss of his mother.

Again, Abraham's servant fell to his knees and thanked the Lord, our God for His help.

Do we remember to thank God, no matter how small or large our blessings are?

Abraham married again and bore many children by his new wife Keturah. Yet Abraham willed everything he owned to Isaac. However, he gave gifts to the sons of his concubines and sent them off into the east away from Isaac. Shortly afterwards, Abraham died.

After Abraham's death, God poured out rich blessings upon Isaac.

Isaac was forty years old when he married Rebecca and Rebecca who was also barren as her mother-in-law Sarah was before God blessed her with Isaac. None-the-less, Isaac pleaded with God, even after many years of marriage he still was asking God to give Rebecca a child.

Because Isaac was a man full of faith and he had pleaded with God so earnestly, God doubled the blessing for Isaac and Rebecca, and she became pregnant with a set of twins.

Rebecca cried out, "It seems as though children are fighting each other inside of me." So she asked the Lord about it.

Then the Lord revealed to her, "The sons in your womb shall become two rival nations. One will be stronger than the other; and the older shall be a servant to the younger!

The two boys were born. The first was born with reddish hair all over his body, so they called him Esau. Then the other twin was born with his hand on Esau's heel! So they called him Jacob. (Meaning "Grabber).

Jacob and Esau were the next two Bible characters we have heard so much about.

One of the best known men of the Bible was Joseph, Jacob and Rachel's first born and was born after Jacob was old also. Joseph was the son with the coat of many colors. His brothers except for the younger brother Benjamin resented him.

Jacob in all had twelve sons. Israel (Jacob's name had been changed to Israel) sent Joseph to see how his brothers were doing; they had been gone for quite some time tending Jacob's flocks.

When Joseph's brothers saw him coming, they recognized him from a distance "Here comes that dreamer," they said, "Let's kill him and throw him in a deep pit! We can tell our father that a wild animal has eaten him." But Reuben came to Joseph's rescue, "Let's not kill him and have a guilty conscience. Let's not be responsible for his death? After all, he is our brother!" Reuben was secretly planning to help Joseph escape and bring him back to Jacob, their father.

After Reuben departed from them, some traders were approaching Joseph's brothers, so the brothers quickly pulled Joseph out of the well where they had placed him and sold him to the traders for twenty pieces of silver.

As we know, Reuben was not with the others when Joseph was sold to the traders. When Reuben returned to the well to get Joseph out of the well, Joseph wasn't there. Reuben ripped at his clothes in anguish and frustration until finally, the other brothers told him what had happened and then they plotted a plan to tell Israel (Jacob).

When Joseph arrived in Egypt as a captive of the Ishmaelite traders, he was purchased from them by Potiphar, an Egyptian and a member of the personal staff of Pharaoh, the king of Egypt. Potiphar was the captain of the king's bodyguards and also his chief executioner.

Potiphar noticed that the Lord greatly blessed Joseph. Everything Joseph did in the home of his master, he did successfully and Potiphar noticed also that the Lord was with Joseph in a very special way. So Joseph became his favorite of all.

After a few needless episodes again in Joseph's life, eventually he was presented with the second highest position over all of Egypt.

And as the story goes, for several generations that is where he and his family dwelled. They were known as the children of Israel, better yet, known as the Israelites and they became a powerful people.

When Joseph died, his last wish where to be buried was to be buried in the land of Canaan, the Promised Land. Therefore, he was carried out under the leadership of Moses and Joshua many years later.

Chapter V

New Testament Beginning Continued

MOSES

Moses was born many years later, after Joseph died. And there was a new ruler on the throne in Egypt. He was the Pharaoh and immediately, he began persecuting Joseph's people like never before. He told his people, "These Israelis' are becoming too many so, let's figure out a way to put an end to their inhabitants flare-up. If we don't, and war breaks out, they will join our enemies and fight against us.

So the Egyptians made slaves of the Israelites and put heartless taskmasters over them.

It is obvious that this Pharaoh undid all that Joseph had done for Egypt and life under this Pharaoh's rule was just unbearable. The merciless treatment was wearing them down under the heavy burdens as they were building the supply cities, Pithorn and Ramses. The new Pharaoh was just inhuman. The Israelites' lives were unjust and unbearable but, they continued to multiply despite this harsh treatment. This ruler was so controlling that he had the boldness to attempt to reduce the population of the Israelites in Egypt by instructing the Hebrew midwives, Shiphrah and Puah to kill all Hebrew boys as soon as they were born.

However, Moses' mother saw that her baby was an unusually beautiful baby that she under no circumstances could give him up so she hid him at home for three months. Then when she could no longer hide him, she made a little boat from papyrus reeds, waterproofed it with tar then placed the baby in it. She laid the little boat and the baby that was in it among the reeds along the edge of the Nile River.

The baby's sister watched from a distance to see what would happen to her baby brother.

As God would have it, the little boat got caught in the reeds and one of Pharaoh's daughters was coming down to the river to bathe. She and her maids were walking along the river bank when she noticed the little boat among the reeds so she sent one of her maids to bring the little boat to her. When she opened it, there was a baby. Her heart went out to this beautiful baby that was just beginning to cry. This touched her heart.

"He must be one of the Hebrew children!" she said.

Quickly the baby's sister approached Pharaoh's daughter and asked her, "Shall I go and find one of the Hebrew women to nurse the baby for you?"

"Yes, please do!" Pharaoh's daughter replied. So the little girl ran home and got her mother.

"Take this child home and nurse him for me," Pharaoh's daughter instructed the baby's mother, who was now hired as the baby's nurse, "and I will pay you well!" she said. So the mother took the baby home and gladly nursed him.

Later, when the child was older, the baby's mother, also who was his hired nurse brought him back to Pharaoh's daughter at the royal Palace and he became the princess's son.

So Pharaoh's daughter, the princess, named the young child Moses. This name means "to draw out" because she had drawn him out of the water.

Even in today's time you can't help but see and feel all this that had happened was God's Will and His plans. To top it all off, God allowed Pharaoh's daughter to choose Mirian, Moses' sister to select a Hebrew nurse to take care of him. And the selected Hebrew nurse was his own mother. Now, only God does things like that.

As time went on, Moses learned that he was one of God's chosen. He was called a Hebrew or an Israelite. And as he grew older he became unhappy at the cruel treatment his people were receiving from the Egyptians.

At the age of forty, Moses made the decision to defend God's people and give up all the finery of the palace. Moses had fled to the land of Midian to live there for another forty years for fear for his life. So, in the land of Midian he lived in the home of Reuel and he became a shepherd. Reuel gave him one of his girls, Zipporah, to be his wife and in that union, they had a baby and named him Gershom, meaning "foreigner because Moses said, "I am a stranger in a foreign land.

One day as Moses was tending the flock of his father-in-law Jethro, the priest of Midian, out at the edge of the desert near Horeb, the mountain of God; suddenly the angel of God appeared to him as a flame of fire in a bush. And Moses noticed that the bush wasn't burnt to a crisp by the fire.

He cautiously went toward the bush to investigate, and then God called out to him, "Moses! Moses!"

"Here am I Lord."

"Don't come any closer," God told him. "Take off your shoes, for you are standing on Holy ground. I am the God of your fathers, the God of Abraham, Isaac, and Jacob."

Moses covered his face with his hands because he was afraid to look at God.

Then the Lord told him, "I have seen the deep sorrows of my people in Egypt, and I have heard their pleas concerning their cruel taskmasters. I will take them out of Egypt away from the Egyptians into a good land, a large land, a land 'flowing with milk and honey'—the land where the Canaanites, Hittites, Amorites, Perizzites, Hivites, and Jebusites live. "Now you go to Pharaoh, and demand that he let my people go.

At this point, as God gave him those instructions, Moses began to reason with God with excuses why he wasn't the person for a job like that!

God ignored his pleas and told that He would be with him.

But Moses continued to question about what God was telling him to do. He asked God, "If I go to the people of Israel and tell them that their fathers' God has sent me, they will ask, 'Which God are you talking about?' What shall I tell them?"

"Just say, 'I Am has sent me!" God, the Supreme replied. And a more detailed instructions and conversation continued between God and Moses.

Still Moses said, "They won't believe me! They won't do what I tell them to do. They'll say, 'The Lord never appeared to you!"

The Lord, our God still continued to show Moses many things to do beginning with the shepherd's own rod and with having an aid, Aaron with him.

Of course God knew that Pharaoh would be ridiculous as Moses and Aaron went before him with the nine plagues. Pharaoh asked Moses and Aaron at the first encounter with them, "who is the Lord that I should obey His Voice?" Moses and Aaron continued to do as God directed having the faith that God had something in mind. And He did.

Moses with Aaron his brother as his spokesman had the greatest work of his life accomplished leading God's people out of bondage from the Egyptians.

God had promised that after the last plague, the tenth plague, Pharaoh would surely let His people go. But before He allowed the last plague to come upon Pharaoh and the Egyptians, He wanted to be sure His people, were protected.

Let's take a break!

Can you see where I am going with this story and why the History is so important to know at this point?

Here have another cup of tea and let's continue.

As we left off, God wanted to be sure His people, were protected so He instructed each Israelite family to kill a lamb and sprinkle the blood on the top and sides of the doorframes. He had this done so when God would see the Blood, He would pass over that house. Therefore, He would not destroy the first born male or first born male animal of that household. God's people, the Israelites, would be spared that gruesome pain Pharaoh and the Egyptians were about to experience.

Notice, the blood of a Lamb saved the Israelites from death, just as the blood of Jesus; the Lamb of God saves us from our sins today.

Chapter VI

New Testament Beginning continues

THE MOSAIC AGE

"The Mosaic Age" is named after Moses. God gave the Old Testament law to the Jews through Moses.

Remember Miriam, Moses Sister, she led God's people in joyful singing and dancing when they were freed from the Egyptians.

Their freedom was as we are today.

Those who have learned and do God's Will are then delivered from the slavery of sin and are freed.

Sometimes you have to shake your head when it comes to humans. Take for instance, after Moses first assured the Israelites that the Lord will fight for them and they wouldn't have to lift a finger, they still gave a deaf ear to what was spoken and even when things was proven, yet they constantly and totally ignored what Moses told them each time things weren't going the way they thought things should go or if things weren't the way they wanted.

The first human ungratefulness is when God harden Pharaoh's heart and Pharaoh led the chase in his chariot to pursue the people of Israel, because they had taken much of the wealth of Egypt with them as God had directed the Israelites to do. And as the Egyptian army was approaching the people of Israel, the Israelites saw them far in the distance, speeding after them and they were terribly frightened and cried out to the Lord to help them. And then they turned against Moses, whining, "Have you brought us out here to die in the desert because there were not enough graves for us in Egypt? Why did you make us leave Egypt?

Can't you see the resemblance of us today?

See how easy they forget how God used Moses to take them out of their bondage.

The next ugly attitude of the Israelites was later when Moses led the people of Israel on from the Red Sea, and they moved out into the wilderness of shur and were there three days without water.

When they arrived at Marah, they couldn't drink the water because it was bitter. Then the people turned against Moses again, "Must we die of thirst?" they demanded to know.

Of course God came to their rescue as usual. He told Moses to tell them that He was with them and so He gave them sweet water.

But the point is and what is so amazing is, how people so easily forget God and put their faith and trust in humans and not God, the God that gave them life.

Even with us today we should learn from their lack of caring and their self-will. We must learn to hunger and thirst after righteousness Matthew 5:6 reads: Blessed *are* those who hunger and thirst for righteousness, for they shall be filled. NKJV

The worst of their human lack of loyalty to God is when Moses came down from the mountain with the tablets of the Ten Commandments that God had written while Moses was on top of the mountain communicating with God, and the people were down below worshipping the golden calf. Moses was so upset when he saw this; in fact, he was so angered that he broke the tablets of the Ten Commandments that God had written with His own Finger.

It is about time humans realized that they aren't the ones in control—God is the one in control and disobedience to God, I repeat, always have consequences. Now because of the people's ignorance and lack of caring, Moses had to pay the consequences when he let his anger get the better of him and the consequences for him after all the trials and tribulations he and the Israelites had gone through, when he struck the rock in anger, disobeying God when God had told Moses to speak to the rock, caused him not be able to cross over into the Promised Land.

So you see, it does not matter what your position is in life, if you are being disobedient or not listening to God's Will, there always will be consequences.

Another example to prove that this is really so is when Moses was on the mountain with God, these people had made themselves a god. They were worshiping a golden calf. Moses was enraged, so enraged that he instructed them to ground the golden calf to a fine powder and he then sprinkled the fine power into their drinking water. And the three thousand men, who refused to drink the water and did not repent of the idolatry, breaking the second commandment, were put to death.

It took another forty years before Moses went up to Mt. Sinai and received another set of Ten Commandments. But, it was so sad that the ungrateful, disobedient Israelites caused Moses to give a statement like this saying, "After all God in all of Heaven or earth has done for us, the Lord was angry with me because of you." As I told you, Moses had struck the rock when God told him to speak to it.

When I read about God telling Moses, "to go to the top of Mount Pisgah," where he could look out in every direction, and there he would see the land in the distance where his foot would never touch. "But you shall not cross the Jordan River," God told Moses, I could have cried with great pain because that is as plain as the nose on my face, God means business. Being obedient means exactly what it say, be obedient. God is the Creator. People are more obedient to their employer more than they are to God . . . think about that.

These unruly people caused Moses such unfair pain for the second time.

Doesn't that just break your heart and people can cause havoc in our lives today too! We must cling to God and not let the ignorant ones that allowed Satan to have a foot hold on them and give us unwarranted stress.

This shows us, regardless what others do; do not lose your cool. Be slow to anger. instead walk the straight and narrow road as best as you humanly know how. Meaning be Christ like in all that you do, regardless how stupid others may act, just because they willingly let Satan get a hold on them. Don't let Satan steal your joy!

That is a shame what happened to Moses after all that time. May I emphasize once more? We should be careful in what we do and say and not allow another human being disillusion us and lead us astray.

These Ten Commandments were the basics of God's laws for the Jewish people during the Mosaic Age. When Moses gave these laws that were specifically for them, called the Old Testament law, he then told them that God would rise up another prophet.

The first House of worship that was ordained by the Heavenly Father was the Tabernacle.

The Bible teaches that the Tabernacle was like some kind of tent type structure.

The twelve tribes of Israelites were camped around it in the courtyard.

How people were then compared to us today: Continuously at that time, there was a pillar of fire at night and a pillar of cloud during the day that hovered over the tabernacle to symbolize to the Israelites of God's presence. But today, God Himself dwells by faith in the hearts of Christians.

And here is another example that God means business when He instructs us to do something, even today.

Now there were two Old Testament Priests Naiad and Abu and they were hardheaded men. While offering incense, they were burned to death by fire from Heaven as a punishment. You see God had commanded a special fire to be used in the Jewish Worship but they got fire from elsewhere, and substituted it from what God had commanded.

This is another great example of man's will and God's Will. This should teach us to worship God only as He directs us in His Word, the Bible rather than according to our own choices that He allows us to have. God does not beg us to worship Him. He doesn't have to. He gives us the choice to hear His Will and obey it if we choose to.

That brings us back to another example. Now as mentioned, in the Old Testament, the priests burned incense as the Law of Moses directed and the priests were only appointed from among the Levi Tribe.

Today in the Christian Age, the Bible teaches that every Christian is a priest.

Burning incense as a worshipping tool to God was strictly an Old Testament practice.

God does not and never has authorized us to do that as Christians in the New Testament.

We must grow in grace and in the knowledge of our Lord and Savior, Jesus Christ. God tell us to pray without ceasing, meaning do not stop praying. In other words, pray all the time for every thing and everybody. That's what Jesus Christ would do and if we love God as we say we do, we would want to be Christ like.

Another order of worship that was practiced in the Old Testament which is the old covenant meaning an agreement with God, and in the New Testament known as the New covenant also an agreement with God is the free-will offering.

The Tabernacle was furnished elaborately by the free-will offering of God's people. God's people gave so generously that Moses had to stop them for giving so much. Today, the Lord's Church in this Christian Age is to be supported by free-will offering too! And in reality, the Christians should give more freely today than in the days of the Israelites. After all, God has given us so much more, including the gift of Jesus Christ, His Son to save us from the depths of punishment!

Now, let us discuss this candlestick worship that they had in the tabernacle and its meaning. The candlestick supported seven lamps and they were lit every evening as part of the Old Testament worship.

In the New Testament, that is today's time, God chose not to use the lamps and candlesticks—instead His Word is sufficient. The Holy Bible is the lamp to light our souls in His New Testament Church. All what is required of the Christians of today is to study His Word daily so we can learn what pleases Him. We study to know His Will because we receive light from God. We must know the foundation of our Faith which should be no different from what the apostles taught, believed and was baptized into the very beginning of the Church on Pentecost AD 32-33 Acts 2:38 reads: Peter replied, "Repent and be baptized, every one of you, in the name of Jesus Christ for the forgiveness of your sins. And you will receive the gift of the Holy Spirit.

Next, let's talk about the showbread they used in the Old Testament and its meaning. Showbread was another tool used in the first Tabernacle in the Old Testament worship. God had this bread eaten only by priest as part of their ritual and it was replaced every Saturday (Sabbath Day).

Today Christians do not use what is called Showbread; instead the Lord's Supper is taken every Sunday called the Lord's Day by the Christians, which is the first day of the week. This is done in remembrance of Jesus Christ's Death and how He died for our sins. Let me remind you again, Christians are priests according to the New Testament.

Looking inside the Tabernacle! We have read about the Tabernacle as being an elaborate tent. It was divided into two rooms. The Holy Place is the first room and the back room was called the Holy of Hollies. In the Old Testament, the High Priest was the only human allowed in this room, the Holy of Hollies and he had to be the eldest male descendent of the family of Aaron.

We also read about the Altar of incense, the candlestick and the showbread which were all contained in the first room. In the Holy of Holies, there was a Veil and the High Priest was the only human to enter inside the Veil only one time every year to make a sin offering for himself and for the people.

It is so different for us today because our High Priest is Jesus Christ and He is the only Mediator between God and humans. Therefore, there's no separate priesthood of men.

Inside the Holy of Hollies was a wooden chest that was overlaid with gold called "the Ark of the Covenant?" It held the original Ten Commandments written on stone. A pot of manna that never spoiled and Aaron's rod that he carried that astonishingly budded overnight. On top of the ark was the "Mercy Seat." This is the place where the

High Priest came yearly under the Mosaic system to be in the presence of God to sprinkle blood of an animal as an offering for atonement for his and the people's sins. But, you see now, our High Priest shed His own blood once and for all for our sins.

The blood of Goats and calves cannot save us. Only Jesus' own blood has obtained eternal redemption for us. Since Jesus' blood obtained eternal redemption, then His death on the cross was the end of animal sacrifices.

Under the Law of Moses, the Priest was required to wash in a basin made of brass before entering the Tabernacle.

Today, we must be washed and cleansed by being immersed in the watery grave of baptism before God allows us to be in His Spiritual Household, the Church.

Let's take a Break!

I've had enough tea . . . let's have some ice water instead and have a good stretch and get back to this wonderful business at hand.

Okay, getting down to the real meaning about how the Lord established the New Testament Church. You see, Christians today, the New testament Church, diligently follow the pattern of worship of the first century Christians and the Apostles. The Scriptures teaches us that the doctrines and commandments of men's worship are worthless, for humans teach their man made laws instead of those from God. Matthew 15:9 reads: They worship me in vain; their teachings are merely human rules. In addition to this, at that time, the Jews being ignorant of God's righteousness, and going about to establish their own righteousness had not submitted themselves to the righteousness of God.

In Romans 10:3 explains more clearly. It reads: Since they did not know the righteousness of God and sought to establish their own, they did not submit to God's righteousness. In other words, the Jews did not understand that Jesus Christ had died to make them right with God. Instead they allowed themselves to put blinders on and humans of today are doing likewise, making themselves follow what they think is right in their eyesight to gain God's approval by keeping the Jewish laws and customs, but that is not God's way of Salvation.

So with these thoughts in mind, It should be recognized that in order to be confident that we are worshiping according to God's Plan and not the human's way of thinking, we must follow the design of worship that God made and what was practiced by the first Christians as in the scriptures, the Holy Bible written by inspired men of God. And then only follow the same way of worship as the early Christians in AD33 without adding anything to God's Instructions or subtracting anything from it. As it is written in Ephesians 1:22-23, It reads: and God placed all things under His (Jesus) feet and appointed Him to be head over everything for the Church, which is His Body, the fullness of Him who fills everything in every way.

Referring back to the Tabernacle, a lesson is learned. When God's people traveled, they took the Tabernacle with them. But it wasn't too long before they learned that the Tabernacle worship could not be a substitute for obedience. God had to show them again that their rebellion against Him would not be acceptable. They had become sinful and wicked once again when they were travelling near Edom.

Because of exhibiting their sinful nature, God sent poisonous snakes among them and so many of the people died as the results. As usual when their backs were against the wall, they called upon God for deliverance. This time, God told Moses to make a fiery Serpent and set it on a pole. But, God didn't remove the poisonous snakes, none-the-less, as always our merciful God and a loving Father made a way for the people to be healed, those who had been bitten by the snakes.

God today, does not take away temptation, but He lifted Jesus Christ up on the cross so that we might be healed from our sins.

We must remember these are the same people's descendants we are talking about who inherited the Land of Canaan. This land was also called "the Promise." because God had promised Abraham that his people would inherit the land. However, it was forty long years before the descendants reached this land for the very reason that they had disloyal hearts throughout all the journeys.

Talking about God meaning what He says, let's look further into Moses striking the rock. That is always a good example. Although

Moses was a good man, God-fearing and all, he still had to be punished for displaying his anger and disobeying God when He struck the rock in a rage. And for not being obedient, Moses wouldn't be allowed to go to the Promised Land because of his sin; Our God still had mercy on His beloved Moses and let him view the land from all angles. Moses, felt good just to know God was real and to see the promise land after such a long journey and unpredictable changes, he was truly grateful. Moses then climbed up to Mt. Nebo and died.

This alone, should teach us that God is not something to play around with. I don't want to be in the Dog House with God, meaning on the wrong side of God. I want to be a twinkle in His eye, how about you?

Even though, it was an unpleasant feeling for Joshua, he was now the children of Israel's new leader so he didn't waste any time. He sent two spies into the land to prepare for conquering it. After the spies reported the condition of the land and its peoples, Joshua made immediate plans to cross the Jordan River into the Promised Land.

By now we should know that God takes care of His Children especially when things look hopeless, besides that is what He has always done and said He would do. For example: when God told the priests to carry the Ark into the river of Jordan which was flooded. The water had raised high at this time, but the Lord told Joshua, "I will give you great honor, so that all Israel will know that I am with you just as I was with Moses.

When the priests who carried the Ark touched the water with their feet; the river stopped flowing as though held back by a dam and immediately as their foot touched the water, God again, as He had done with the red sea, divided the water and all the Israelites crossed on dry land.

So, after forty years of wandering, only Joshua and Caleb of the original generation that had escaped slavery from the Egyptians crossed over into the Promised Land.

Chapter VII

The Judges and the Kings

After Joshua's death for three hundred years the Israelites were ruled by leaders called Judges. The Judges and the military were their leaders from then on.

And wouldn't you know it the Israelites did evil in the eyes of the Lord again so the Lord sold them into the hands of Jabin king of Canaan. The commander of his army was Sisera who was cruel and oppressed the Israelites for twenty years and of course, the Israelites cried out loud to the Lord for help. As usual again, God came to their rescue and when they repented of their idolatry, He delivered them from the Canaanites through the leadership of Deborah, a woman prophetess.

God sees to it that the last Judge of Israel would be Samuel. His mother Hannah prayed to God for him and God answered her prayer. She also promised God that she would dedicate him to the Lord's service all his life. And she kept her promise to God.

While her son was still very young, she took him miles away to the Priest Eli. Eli trained him and used him in the service of the Lord. But as a mother, she couldn't completely give her baby up; each year when she went to the Tabernacle she took him a new coat. This was her way of showing love for her son that she had prayed for. And Samuel became the first in a long line of prophets who preached God's message to the people.

When Samuel grew older, he appointed his sons as judges, but they became corrupt too! The people of Israel took this to be a reason to demand a king so they could be like all the other nations. You can see that they were not satisfied with just being God's chosen people.

Samuel was upset by their demand, but when he prayed to God, God told him: "It is not you they have rejected; they have rejected me, as they have done from the day I brought them up out of Egypt until this day, forsaking me and serving other gods."

Can't you imagine God throwing His Hands up in the air in disgust? No! Neither can I that would be the way humans think. None-the-less, God granted their request as they continuously begged for a king.

God told Samuel that a young Benjamite would approach him, who is the son of Kish and that Samuel was to anoint him king. Therefore, Samuel showed special favor to Saul, of which Saul considered himself unworthy. But still being obedient to God, Samuel anointed Saul king.

At that time there wasn't a man who could be compared with Saul for the job of being king. Not only that, he was handsomely built with outstanding courage, yet, a humble man and not vain. So now Saul was the first King of the Israelites.

But Samuel told the Israelites all the words of the Lord to the people who were asking him for a king. He said, "This is what the king who will reign over you will do: He will take your sons and make them serve his chariots and horses even run in front of them. Some will be assigned to be commanders of thousands and commanders of fifties, and others to plow his ground and reap his harvest, and still others to make weapons of war and equipment for his chariots.

Your daughters will be cooks, bakers and perfumers. He will take the best of your fields and vineyards and olive groves and give them to his attendants. He will take a tenth of your grain and of your vintage and give it to his officials and attendants.

Your menservants and maidservants and the best of your cattle and donkeys he will take for his very own use. Not only that, he will take a tenth of your flocks, and all of you will become his slaves. When that day comes, you will cry out for relief from the king you have chosen, and the Lord will not answer you that day as He has done so often before.

As a King, Saul was powerful and successful as he led the army that conquers. He became very popular among the people but soon he began to lose his humbleness and became arrogant and disobedient to God's orders.

This was the consequences of the Israelites for wanting an earthy man for their king and leader to guide them. This also showed them the fulfilling of the scriptures Samuel had told them about.

While Saul was still on the throne and was getting farther and farther from God, God finally rejected Saul. So for the second King for Israel, God chose David.

David was a young shepherd boy and the son of Jesse. David was courageous and had a sincere love and deep faith for God.

When God directed Samuel to anoint David as King, Saul was still on the throne at that time, God made it known that the Lord sees not as man see; for man look on the outward appearance, but the Lord look on the Heart." And although David was the youngest of his older brothers, he still was anointed to be the new king and he didn't hesitate to serve the Lord and he also became very popular with the people. He was so popular with them that they chanted, "Saul has killed his thousands and David his tens of thousands.

Saul became very jealous and made attempts to kill David. Finally after forty years, Saul killed himself and young David was then the ruler of Israel. David also reigned over Israel for forty years, seven of them in Hebron and thirty-three in Jerusalem. And he was known as "the man after God's own Heart." David wrote many Psalms too! After David's death, his young son Solomon was anointed the third king.

God told the young man Solomon to ask for any blessing he'd like. Young Solomon felt inadequate to rule over Israel so he prayed and asked God, "Give me and understanding heart (Mind) so that I can govern your people well and know the difference between what is right and what is wrong. For by myself I am not able to carry such a heavy responsibility." God was pleased with Solomon's request and was glad that Solomon had asked for wisdom. So in a dream God said to him, "Because you have asked for wisdom in governing my people, and haven't asked for a long life or riches for yourself or the defeat of your enemies—I'll give you what you asked for! I will give you a wiser mind than anyone else has ever had or ever will have! And also, I will give you what you didn't ask for—such as: riches and respect with admiration! And no one in the entire world will be as rich and famous as you will be for the rest of your life!" Then God concluded, "And I will give you a long life if you follow me and obey my laws as your father David did." Solomon had wide-range of interests and he was the author of proverbs and he wrote many songs. And kings from many lands sent their ambassadors to him for his advice.

So God did answer his prayer by giving him wisdom above any other man.

As you may remember, five hundred Years prior, Moses had built a Tabernacle. Now God had put Solomon in charge with building His Temple in Jerusalem to replace the existing Tabernacle Moses built. The skilled men took seven years to construct it and it was fabulous. King Solomon selected laborers from all parts of Israel—thirty thousand men.

Solomon ruled Israel wisely for forty prosperous years and his name was favorably known.

When the queen of Sheba heard how pleasingly God had blessed Solomon with wisdom, she decided to search his mind and test him with some tough questions. Solomon answered all her inquisitive questions; nothing was too difficult for him, for God had given him the right answers every time. God gave Solomon such great wisdom, the Book of Proverbs is filled with his wisdom.

Solomon came to one conclusion out of all his challenges and we all should adopt it, "The whole duty of man (Humans) is to Fear God and keep his commandments.

But even Solomon failed. King Solomon married many other women besides the Egyptian princess. Many of them came from nations where idols were being worshiped. Even though the Lord our God had clearly instructed His people not to marry into those nations, because those women should they married them would cause them to stray and get them started worshiping their gods. Yet Solomon did it anyway.

Solomon did what clearly was wrong and didn't follow God as his father David did. He even built a temple on Mount of Olives, across the valley from Jerusalem for these foreign wives to use for burning incense and sacrificing to their gods.

God was very angry with Solomon concerning his conduct, for now Solomon was no longer interested in serving God of Israel who had appeared to him twice to warn him specifically against worshiping other gods.

But Solomon didn't listen. Then God said to him, "Since you have not kept our agreement and have not obeyed my laws, I will take the kingdom away from you and your family and give it to someone else. But for the sake of your father David, I won't do this while you are still alive. I will take the kingdom away from your son. But! I will let him be king of just one tribe, for the sake of David and for the sake of Jerusalem, my chosen city.

This is scary! We should take notice how devout and strong a man Solomon was with all the wisdom in the world and he still allowed material things and other human beings change his course in life.

Solomon forgot what he had told the Israelites and to us too! "The whole duty of man (humans) is to Fear God and keeps his commandments.

From Saul to Solomon, the Israelites had been completely united. But after Solomon's death, Satan stepped in again.

The Israelites split into two separate nations becoming Judah and Israel who distrusted each other.

This is how it happened.

Rehoboam, King Solomon's son, had his inauguration and all Israel came for the ceremony after the King's death.

Jeroboam was still in Egypt where he had fled from King Solomon, when he heard about the coming event from his friends who urged him to attend the inauguration. He then joined the rest of Israel at Shechem and became the ringleader in getting the people to make certain demands upon Rehoboam, Solomon's son.

"Your father was a hard master," they told Rehoboam. "We don't want you as our King unless you promise to treat us better than he did.

Rehoboam told them to "Come back in three days" for an answer. Then Rehoboam talked it over with the old men who had counseled his father Solomon.

They told him "Give them a pleasant answer and agree to do good by them, and then they would desire for you to be their king forever. But Rehoboam refused the old men's advice and went to the young men whom he had grown up with. Of course they told him to say, "If you think my father was hard on you, well, I'll be harder! So the new king refused the people's demands. (But the Lord's hand was in this—He caused the new king to do this in order to fulfill His promise).

When the people heard the news that the new king would be harder than King Solomon, they shouted, "Down with David and all his relatives! Let's go home! Let Rehoboam be king of his own family!" And they all deserted him except for the tribe of Judah, who remained loyal to Rehoboam as their King as was told would happen.

As soon as the people of Israel learned of Jeroboam's return to Egypt, he was asked to come before all the people and there he was made king of Israel. Only the tribe of Judah continued under the kingship of the family of David.

And that is how the division began. Ten of the twelve tribes rebelled and established the northern part of Palestine. This was the Kingdom of Israel with Jeroboam as its King.

Rehoboam continued to rule over two tribes and they became the Kingdom of Judah.

Jerobam did not want the ten tribes to return to Jerusalem. He thought that the people would become friendly with King Rehoboam and then they would kill him and ask Rehoboam to be their king. Jeroboam had already built the city of Shechem in the hill country of Ephraim and it became his capital. Next he built Penuel.

On the advice of the counselors, Jeroboam, their king, made two golden calves and then told the people, "It's too much trouble to go to Jerusalem to worship; from now on these idols will be your gods. He even lied and told them that those golden calves recued them from their captivity in Egypt! One golden calf he set up in Bethel, and the other in Dan. And in doing this, it was a sin, a big sin. The people went as far as Dan to worship! Jeroboam built shrines and appointed priests, even though they were not Levites. He instituted a festival on the fifteenth day of the eighth month and offered sacrifices on the altar. He even sacrificed to the calves he had made.

Soon the Israelites were known as a group of Idolatry committing people.

Judah and Israel remained divided until they both were captured by their enemies.

Chapter VIII

The Prophets

The prophets were teachers God inspired and He sent these prophets to call His people back to His Worship.

Isaiah was one of the greatest prophets that ever lived. He lived about seven hundred and fifty years before Jesus Christ left Heaven and came to earth. Isaiah told of the time God would establish a New Kingdom. It would not be just for the Israelites but, for all nationalities. He told all about Jesus Christ in detail. Also Isaiah's predictions and details about Jesus' life on earth came true and Isaiah became known as the Mosaic Prophet.

Daniel was another God fearing man. Daniel worshiped God even after being captured and was told not to worship God. So, he was thrown in a lion's den as punishment for worshipping God, but God closed the mouths of the lions and Daniel was safe.

Daniel let it be known that the Kingdom set up by God, will itself endure forever.

Gabriel A Busy Bee

It was now time for God to go into action again.

He began to fulfill His promise by choosing one of His Angels named Gabriel.

Gabriel's mission was to go to Zacharias, the Priest and tell Zacharias and his wife that they were going to have a son and they must name him John.

Their son John is the one who would prepare the way for the coming of the Lord.

In a way, it is like announcing a celebrity, just as we do for a president or some dignitary before their actual appearance.

About six months later, God sent Gabriel to Nazareth. Gabriel gave a message from God to a young virgin named Mary. "You will be with child and give birth to a son, and you are to give him the name Jesus," Gabriel said, repeating the message as God directed him to do.

At that time, Mary was engaged to a man named Joseph.

God knew Joseph's heart and Mary's and He knew once Joseph had heard the details, he would understand and be obedient and that is why God chose them. Then because of knowing their hearts, God sent and Angel to Joseph who assured him that the woman he wished to marry was still a virgin and pure, even though she was with child conceived by the Holy Spirit.

And Mary continued to remain pure until after the birth of Jesus Christ. She then had other children by Joseph, her husband.

And as the story goes, Caesar Augustus, the Roman Emperor, authorized that a census should be taken throughout the nation. The census was taken when Quirinius was governor of Syria. Everyone was required to return to his inherited home for this registration and because Joseph was a member of the royal line, he had to go to Bethlehem in Judea, King David's ageless home.

Joseph took his fiancée Mary, who was pregnant on this long journey to Bethlehem, and when they reached their destination, the time was approaching for the baby to be born.

The little town of Bethlehem was so crowded that there was no room for them anywhere. And it was getting closer and closer for Baby Jesus to make His entry into this world. Oh! Poor Joseph! Can't you imagine him panicking? He had no hospital floor to pace and he didn't have the time to pace at all. The Baby is ready to be born.

In the meantime because of the quick need, the Innkeeper allowed them only one place he could think of.

Joseph and Mary had no other choice but to spend the night in a stable where Mary gave birth to her firstborn, a son named Jesus. She wrapped Him in swaddling (tucked in) cloths and placed Him in a manger, because there was no room for them in the inn.

Certainly, God planned it that way. This was our first lesson in humbleness.

This Baby Jesus is the Son of God who had existed with God the Father and now had come to earth to be our Savior. Jesus has no human father.

Did you know, our entire life depends on Jesus Christ, our Lord and Savior and we should feel that it is a huge privilege? To know about Jesus Christ being our Savior leads to contentment of heart and peace within. We all will die, so think about where you will spend eternity.

Chapter IX

A Magnificent Man

In the Scriptures little is known about Jesus growing up except that He was full of wisdom. And when Jesus was twelve years old, His knowledge amazed the scholars of the law in the Temple.

He let it be known that He was about His Father's Business to His mother when she had expressed how worried she and Joseph were about His whereabouts. He didn't worry His mother like that anymore as a child. God, our Heavenly Father was pleased with Him for being considered of their human feelings.

Now this is where it all began. Jesus Christ the Heavenly Being who came down to this earth to be a Perfect Human being and a Magnificent Man for us. Jesus was about thirty—years-old when He began His Ministry.

Earlier, we talked about John the Baptist who prepared the way for the beginning of the Gospel about Jesus Christ, the Son of God as God had planned.

In other words, "Turn from your sins and turn to God . . . for the Kingdom of Heaven is coming soon," John preached. And so John was baptizing in the desert region, a baptism of repentance for the forgiveness of sins. The whole Judean countryside and all the people of

Jerusalem went out to him. Confessing their sins, they were baptized by him in the Jordan River.

John wore clothing made of camel's hair, with a leather belt around his waist, and he ate locusts and wild honey.

This was his message: "With water I baptize those who repent of their sins; but one will come more powerful than I am, He's so powerful that I am not worthy to untie His sandals and He will baptize you with the Holy Spirit.

To fulfill all righteousness and prophecies, Jesus came all the way from Galilee to be baptized by John in the Jordan River.

John didn't want to do it. "This isn't appropriate," he said. "I am the one who needs to be baptized by you.

But Jesus said, "Please do baptize me John, for I must do all that is right.

So John baptized Jesus.

Just as soon as Jesus came up out of the water after John baptized him, the Heavens were opened to Him and John saw the Spirit of God coming down in the form of a Dove. And a voice from Heaven said, "This is my beloved Son, In Him I am well pleased. And God placed all things under Jesus' feet and appointed Him to be head over everything, the fullness of Him who fills everything in every way.

Notice this, Jesus was baptized but not for the reasons we are baptized.

We are baptized for the Remission of Sins. Jesus knew no sin.

Have you really given any thought to the word 'Baptize"? Baptizo is Greek for baptism.

Here is an easy understanding of being Baptized; When Noah and his family boarded the ark, Noah had followed God's commands as God had told him to do and that great flood was the cleansing of the earth. Likewise as we enter the watery grave of being baptized, the act of baptism cleanses our bodies of our sins. Then as we come out of the watery grave we rise as Jesus Christ arouse out of His grave. We rise clean and into a newness of life. All born again as a new born babe in Christ with all our past sins washed away.

That's what represents baptism. Baptism is necessary to do because it is the Will of God and it is a part of His Plan of Salvation.

Jesus was baptized because it was God the Father's Will. Really, Jesus did not need to be baptized but it was for a wonderful obedient example for us to follow.

You and I must be baptized (immerse) for the remission of sins. Reading Acts 2:38 again: Peter replied, "Repent and be baptized, every one of you, in the name of Jesus Christ for the forgiveness of your sins. And you will receive the gift of the Holy Spirit. And also, we are to be Christ like in obedience. I Peter 2:21 says: To this you were called, because Christ suffered for you, leaving you an example that you should follow in His steps. We must obey God, our Heavenly Father if we love Him as we say we do, keeping God's Commandments is also proof that we know and understand His Will.

Reading I John2:3-4 says: We know that we have come to know Him if we keep his commands. Whoever says, "I know Him," but does not do what He commands is a liar, and the truth is not in that person.

That is as plain as plain can get. How much more plainly can it be?

Even though Jesus is the Son of God, He lived and died under the Mosaic Law. Jesus Ministry took place during the Mosaic period. That is the old Law period, as stated earlier, and the laws of Moses. When our Lord and Savior died, so did all the Old Laws, better yet known as the Old covenant (the Old Testament). Now after John baptized Jesus, John saw all what happened with his own two eyes and that made John an eyewitness to Jesus Christ being God's only begotten son with the Holy Spirit in the form of a Dove landing on Jesus and hearing God the Father say, "This is my Beloved Son in whom I am well pleased." John told everyone, "I saw it happen to this man, and I therefore testify that He is the Son of God." John 1:34.

John continued his testimony: "I saw the spirit come down from Heaven as a Dove and lingered on Him. I would not have known Him, except that the One who sent me to baptize with water told me. "He said to me," John nonstop telling all, "The man on whom you see the Spirit come down and remain on Him is He who will baptize with the

Holy Spirit." John eagerly reported "I have seen and I testify that this is the Son of God."

The twelve and Jesus Christ's Mission

Jesus Christ chose twelve men. They had varies occupations and different attitudes. These are the men Jesus Christ chose to be His Apostles. These men believed and trusted in Him. And they are the ones He knew would lead the people and teach them the Good News of Salvation.

Jesus knew He would be returning to our Heavenly Father in Heaven. And that is why the Holy Spirit was sent to guide the Apostles so that they would adequately teach us about the Salvation of Jesus Christ, because He is the only go between God and us. In this way in the New Testament, God gave to us humans a full and complete understanding of His Will.

Jesus came to earth being the only one over qualified to offer Himself for our sins. Jesus said, "I am the Way, the Truth and the Life, no man (human—man or woman) come unto the Father (God) but by Me." (Jesus Christ).

Jesus dying on the Cross fulfilled the prophecy. Many Jews soon accepted Jesus as their Savior as well as some of the gentiles. Our Lord died for us all. Jews and Gentiles (nationalities other than Jews).

Crucifixion

The custom in those days was that the Jewish leaders didn't want the crucified to be hanging on their crosses the next day, which was the Sabbath and that up-coming Sabbath was a very special Sabbath, for it was the Passover. So they asked Pilate to give the orders to break the legs of the men hanging on the crosses to speed up their death; in that way the bodies could be taken down by 5 p.m. that afternoon. So the solders did as ordered and they broke the legs of the two men who were crucified with Jesus; but! When they came to Jesus, they saw that He was already dead, so they didn't break his legs. Instead, one of the soldiers pierced Jesus' side with a spear, bringing a sudden flow of blood and water.

These things happened so that the scripture would be fulfilled as it had been said. "Not one of His bones will be broken.

The Mosaic History and the Old Testament law came to an end when Jesus Christ died.

After Jesus was raised from the dead, He ascended back to the Father (God).

Chapter X

The Purpose

THE CHRISTIAN NOW!

The New Testament in which we now live is a crucial point in our lives. The Pentateuch history of Adam/Eve and the Creation, Noah and the flood, the Mosaic history, (Moses and the law): and the Israelites being led through the Red sea; Jesus Christ giving the Sermon on the Mount, and His death, are all a part of the Old Testament history that has provided the background for our understanding of the New Testament better in this time.

The New Testament is the New Covenant with God the Father and God the Son because Jesus Christ is the messiah who replaced the Old Testament.

The Old Testament and the New Testament, both are "Agreements in its times with God.

The New Testament began after Jesus' death and resurrection. And it will continue until Jesus Christ returns and the time shall be no more.

In other words, now is the time for us to get all our ducks in order, be watchful as well as pray because no one knows when Jesus Christ will come to earth again, not even Jesus Christ Himself. Only the Heavenly Father knows.

God the Father allows His only begotten Son who now sits on His right side with the power and control God the Father had given Him over all things except for the knowledge of His return.

Worshiping God and Jesus Christ weekly, and taking of the Lord's Supper is a spiritual duty and a sacred privilege. But, some view doing this weekly is unnecessary. And some call the Lord's Super communion and they believe that taking the communion monthly is sufficient. Others ask, "How did this practice begin any way and why? And there are some who do not believe that there is any biblical support for worshipping on Sunday either, let alone taking of the Lord's Supper weekly. Although there is no obvious New Testament statement confirming Sunday worship, there are plenty of verses specifying Sunday, the first day of the week, as being special, a day of breaking bread, and gathering of collections.

Here they are: Jesus rose from the dead on the first day of the week Matthew 28:1-7 (After the Sabbath, at dawn on the first day of the week, Mary Magdalene and the other Mary went to look at the tomb.); Mark 16:2 (Very early on the first day of the week, just after sunrise, they were on their way to the tomb); John 20:1 (Early on the first day of the week, while it was still dark, Mary Magdalene went to the tomb and saw that the stone had been removed from the entrance.). And as we get into communion, (the Lord's Supper) the First Day of the Week will be proven further. Jesus appeared to the disciples on the first day of the week.

John 20:19 reads: On the evening of that first day of the week, when the disciples were together, with the doors locked for fear of the Jewish leaders, Jesus came and stood among them and said, "Peace be with you!"

Further reading: Jesus appeared inside the room to the eleven disciples eight days after the first day of the week. The Jewish way of measuring days meant that it was again Sunday. Notice: the situation is until midnight which is not the Jewish method of measuring days, but the Roman system. And John 20:26 reads: A week later his disciples were in the house again, and Thomas was with them. Though the doors were locked, Jesus came and stood among them and said, "Peace be with you! Paul instructed the congregations of the Lord's Church to put aside contributions on the first day of the week. I Corinthians 16:2

reads: On the first day of every week, each one of you should set aside a sum of money in keeping with your income, saving it up, so that when I come no collections will have to be made.

Jesus taught His disciples about His Kingdom which was soon to come.

It is the foundation of His Kingdom and it is the Truth that He is God's Son.

When Jesus came to the region of Caesarea Philippi, He asked His disciples, "Who do people say the Son of Man is?" They replied, "Some says John the Baptist; others say Elijah; and still others, Jeremiah or one of the prophets.

When Jesus asked His disciples "but whom say ye that I am?" Peter answered, "Thou art the Christ, the Son of the living God.

Jesus praised Peter for accepting the evidence of God and not the thoughts of men. Then Jesus Christ said, "Thou art Peter, and upon this rock, I will build my Church.

In all honesty this is where some people get the mistaken idea that the Church was built on Peter and not on Jesus Christ. But knowing what Paul, the Apostle taught, "For other Foundation can no man lay than that is laid, which is Jesus Christ. As it is written, for no one can lay any foundation other than the one already laid, which is Jesus Christ. Now truly how can such powerful words be misconstrued?

Peter means Peblo or a small pebble or a movable little stone Jesus was referring to Himself, a Firm, Solid Rock that cannot be moved. The Rock upon which the Church is built, the Son of God and that is the heavenly announcement Peter confessed.

In Matthew 15:17 Jesus said to Peter after Peter made his statement, "God has blessed you Simon, son of Jonah, for my Father in Heaven has revealed this to you.

Neither Peter nor John was the Rock or the Corner Stone that has a Solid Foundation.

The King James Version I Peter 2:6 reads: Wherefore also it is contained in the scripture, Behold, I lay in Zion a chief corner stone, elect, precious: and he that believeth on Him shall not be confused.

The International Standard Version I Peter 2:6 reads: This is why it says in Scripture: "Look! I am laying a chosen, precious cornerstone in Zion. The one who believes in Him will never be ashamed.

Both versions are saying: "What a foundation you stand on with Jesus Christ being the cornerstone of the building.

A chief cornerstone is the principal stone on which the corner of the structure rests.

Ephesians 2:20 reads: built on the foundation of the apostles and prophets, with Christ Jesus Himself as the Chief Cornerstone.

Crucifixion Continued

On the day of Jesus Christ's crucifixion, the disciples removed His Body from the cross and lovingly and tenderly laid Jesus in the tomb of a friend.

Some seven hundred and fifty years earlier Isaiah had prophesied that the Roman guards would place a huge stone in front of Jesus Christ's tomb and that guards would be guarding it. They did this because the Romans feared that someone would steal Jesus Christ's body from the tomb and claim that Jesus Christ had risen from the dead as had been prophesied to make sure it would be known indeed that the prophesy was true.

But! Death itself could not hold God's Son. Jesus had to rise from the dead to break the bonds of death.

Because of His resurrection, our sins are forgiven, our life is renewed, our hope is permanent, and our eternity is secured. We are given a new start, a new life, and a new future.

When Jesus Christ broke the bonds of death, surely that was a Great Day for the New Testament Church, Jesus Lives, This act is the Greatest Blessing for us and it gives us a chance to be alive with Him and to be forgiven of our sins that Adam and Eve brought into the world.

God the Father and Jesus made it possible for us to shed ourselves of this guilt of sins. There is no other love But Jesus Christ. There is no other forgiveness but Jesus Christ. And there is no other one that can save our souls, but Jesus Christ.

In the Word of God, the Bible has proven that Jesus Christ is Truly, Truly the Son of God.

After Jesus Christ's Resurrection, He appeared to His disciples often, (a total of forty days at various places) and told them much more about His Kingdom, (His Church). He told them to preach about His Kingdom to the whole world that He died for their sins. And Jesus Christ told them to wait in Jerusalem for the Holy Spirit to come upon them to help them tell the world that the Savior really had died for their sins. Then Jesus Christ blessed them as He began ascending into Heaven and the disciples watched Him disappear into the cloud.

Heavenly Messengers appeared to the apostles and assured them that someday Jesus Christ would return.

Now, I believe this is where man of today (human beings, male and female) misses the mark!

Ephesians 2:19-22 (Bible Verses about the Church, the Body of Christ) reads: Consequently, you are no longer foreigners and aliens, but fellow citizens with God's people and members of God's household, built on the foundation of the apostles and prophets, with Christ Jesus Himself as the chief cornerstone. In him the whole building is joined together and rises to become a holy temple in the Lord. And in him you too are being built together to become a dwelling in which God lives by His Spirit.

All this is to say: Now you are no longer strangers to God and foreigners in Heaven, but you are members of God's very own family citizens of God's country and you belong in God's household with every other Christian. We who believe are carefully joined together with Christ as parts of a beautiful, constantly growing temple for God. And we also are joined with Him and with each other by the Spirit and are part of this dwelling place of God.

You agree now don't you? That Jesus died for the sins of man . . . that Jesus ascended into Heaven to sit on the right hand side of God, the Father Almighty.

But! You yourself or me or any human being cannot pray to God the Father directly because, God let it be known that no one can come to Him but by Jesus Christ. When Jesus Christ died on the cross and rose again, His Kingdom was then established, which is His Church and therefore, we can't go to the Father without first addressing Jesus Christ and certainly not to mother Mary or St. Paul or whoever that did not die for us.

Jesus Christ died for; His followers, His believers who believe He is He. These believers make up His Kingdom. That is who He died for and that is His body that He is the head of. He is the Tree and His Believers are the branches. His death earned Him the right to rule and to reign over everything and God the Father had given Him all authority.

Why is it so difficult for humans to accept the way it is.

After the Apostles watched Jesus ascend into Heaven, they returned to Jerusalem as Jesus had instructed them to do.

Ten days after Jesus ascended into Heaven, Jesus sent the Holy Spirit upon them and it came with a sound from Heaven as a violent wind that filled the whole house where they were sitting. Not only that, they saw what seemed to be forked tongues of fire that set upon each apostle and each apostle spoke in different languages as the spirit enabled them.

Now as only God would have it, there were staying in Jerusalem God-fearing Jews from every nation from all over the world to visit in Jerusalem at this particular time because, it was the Jewish feast of Pentecost. These people were amazed when they heard and understood what was being told about Jesus and His Kingdom in their own language.

After hearing the gospel of Christ, His Church began with three-thousands Jews (Souls if you will) who on that day turned from Judaism to Christ. This was the beginning of the first congregation of the Church of Christ. Christ's Body and His followers are members of His Body; His Church and His only Kingdom that He died for.

Look what Ephesians 1:22-23 says: And God placed all things under His feet and appointed Him to be Head over everything for the

Church, which is His Body, the fullness of Him who fills everything in every way.

And Colossians 1:18 reads: And He is the Head of the Body, the Church; He is the beginning and the firstborn from among the dead, so that in everything He might have the supremacy. Meaning the Church is Christ's Body and the Church has only One Head and that Head belong to Jesus Christ.

Again allow me to repeat, God has given Him, this Jesus full authority in the Church.

I Corinthians 12:12-27 tells us that the Church is Christ's Body—It is One Body with many members, and each member was baptized into the One Body and each member has a function, some more than others but, never-the-less, each member is important.

Let's look at your physical body. Your body has eyes, toes, legs, ears arms, nose, mouth, heart, hands and each member of your body has a function, (talent if you will) but, all these members belong to the one body.

Now when it comes to Jesus Christ and the members of His body, His Church who He is the Head of and the Chief Corner Stone, works together in the same manner as the human physical body. Simple, the Church Body and the Church functions made up of each member and their talents work together as a whole. They work for the Lord using the talents He has given each member of His Body. Some preach the Gospel, some are teachers, some encourage others in everyday life, some serve others, and some are just gifted leaders and most of all, each member is important. There isn't one person (member) more important than the other. They all work together in unity and functions as God planned.

Jesus Christ is simple and humble and His members who are obedient to Him should be likewise.

Remember that the Heavenly Father is our provider. So, don't allow material things to control your life, letting your life be guided by your material possessions and ignoring the guidance of God and His Will.

Place Him first in all areas of your life and most of all, do His Will, not yours. That is all He asks of us.

'Baptism' for a Greater Understanding

Those who had their sins washed away through baptism, immersion, did as Jesus Christ did when He died on the cross. Called the death, burial and resurrection . . . But the difference is that we humans enter the water with sins and our sins are buried at the bottom of the water, called the watery grave. When we rise out of the water we are clean with the pass sins buried and forgotten by God and that is what is meant by a new born babe in Christ Jesus.

Chapter XI

Examining the Kingdom

There are at the least four things that are necessary before any Kingdom can exist, whether it be a Spiritual Kingdom or a physical kingdom.

A physical kingdom is based on the human idea and human standards, as they are considered necessary and to their liking. But! The real, Kingdom purchased with Jesus Christ's own Blood is founded on a Spiritual Foundation.

Of every Kingdom there must be:

A King (Authority figure)

A Headquarters

A Subject

A Law

These are all-necessary for any Kingdom

John 18:36. Reads: Jesus said, "My kingdom is not of this world. If it were, my servants would fight to prevent my arrest by the Jewish leaders. But now my kingdom is from another place.

Jesus Christ's Headquarters is in Heaven and His subjects are those who hear His Gospel correctly, without additions or subtracting. God's Words (the Bible) does not need man's (Human) interpretation. It is Jesus Christ's Spiritual Kingdom. His Church and Jesus Christ have all authority. He's the Head of His Church and it is not governed by any earthly rules and regulations. Besides, any organization, club, etc. that you are voted into, you can easily be voted out of.

Please be aware that anyone who will come to Jesus and accept His terms and not man's terms, and becomes a part of Jesus and His Body who He adds you to, no one can put him/her out of His Body, which is His Church and His believers are members of it.

Only Jesus Himself has the authority to accept or reject. Jesus does not vote you into His Kingdom. He adds you to Himself. Acts 2:38-41. And Jesus will not beg you to choose Him.

Man's thoughts are not God's thoughts. Isaiah 55:8 reads: "For my thoughts are not your thoughts, neither are your ways my ways," said the Lord.

What does the Word Gospel really Mean?

Often we hear people speak of the Gospel but not really giving thought to the contents.

Perhaps it has been a hand me down through the years from childhood. You know, what the old folks say, "If it's good enough for my mother, its good enough for me. Give me that ol' Time religion."

What is that ol' time religion anyway?

With some to them it means that the word Gospel just refers to the Bible in its entirety.

The Gospel is the New Testament's 'Good News', the death, burial and resurrection of Jesus Christ. The New Testament clearly let it be known that the Kingdom of God (the Gospel) and the Salvation of Jesus Christ, is within you. That's how the Lord designed His Church.

People will not be able to point at a building saying, "there it is" because the Kingdom of God is within you. Luke 17:21 (King James Version) reads: And when he was demanded of the Pharisees, when the kingdom of God should come, he answered them and said the kingdom of God cometh not with observation: Neither shall they say, Lo here! or, lo there! for, behold, the kingdom of God is within you. Of course there are buildings used as a meeting place but even so, if the meeting place was at the beach, or someone's back yard, still you will be in God's Kingdom, His Church because His Church is within you! That is those who believe and follow Jesus directions.

The Apostles called the Gospel by various names and you probably will recognize some or have used some of them yourself. I will list some of these various names for you to read and know where they are located: Gospel of God Romans 1:1: reads: Paul, a servant of Christ Jesus, called to be an apostle and set apart for the Gospel of God; 1Thessalonians 2:9 reads: Surely you remember brothers and sisters, our toil and hardship; we worked night and day in order not to be a burden to anyone while we preached the Gospel of God to you, Gospel of Jesus Christ. Romans 15:19 reads: By the power of signs and wonders, through the power of the Spirit of God. So from Jerusalem all the way around to Illyricum, I have fully proclaimed the Gospel of Christ. Galatians 1:6-7 reads:: I am astonished that you are so quickly deserting the one who called you to live in the grace of Christ and are turning to a different gospel—7 which is really no gospel at all. Evidently some people are throwing you into confusion and are trying to pervert the Gospel of Christ. Gospel of the Grace of God, Acts 20:24 reads: However, I consider my life worth nothing to me; my only aim is to finish the race and complete the task the Lord Jesus has given me—the task of testifying to the good news of God's grace.

Gospel of Salvation Ephesians 1:13 reads: And you also were included in Christ when you heard the message of truth, the Gospel of your salvation. When you believed, you were marked in Him with a seal, the promised Holy Spirit. And all these names let us know that Jesus Christ is the Gospel and the life of it. The Gospel is also the message of God and the redemption in and by Jesus Christ. The teaching of Christianity God offered to mankind through His only begotten Son, Jesus Christ.

Proof: Matthew 28:19-20 reads: Go therefore and make disciples of all the nations, baptizing them in the name of the Father and the Son and the Holy Spirit, teaching them to observe all that I commanded you; and lo, I am with you always, even to the end of the age. And Mark 16:15-16 reads: And He said to them, "Go into the entire world and preach the Gospel to all creation. He who has believed and has been baptized shall be saved; but he who has disbelieved shall be Condemned.

Following Jesus is the most important task for us to do in our lives. Being obedient to what He has told us to do in the Bible and the Bible alone which is His Words and directions for us to obey and be His disciples, His followers.

Jesus Christ's Church is not made with Human hands.

The Average subjects.

Who are the average subjects? They are those who do not understand fully God's Word, (the Bible).

In order not to be an average subject we must realize that God's spiritual Kingdom are those who have Faith in Jesus and will submit to Him completely. Accept Jesus Christ as our King and our Master.

This is the Same God who made us, nations and all nationalities.

Now, let's face the true facts, there are two distinctive kingdoms. One belongs to Jesus Christ, God's Son, (God the Father, and God the Son agrees as one). And the second kingdom belongs to Satan. Every living person is a subject and God allows every subject the right to make their own decisions.

But in the case of these two kingdoms we read about in Ephesians 6:12: For our struggle is not against flesh and blood, but against the rulers, against the authorities, against the powers of this dark world and against the spiritual forces of evil in the heavenly realms.

So you see even though we can make our own choices, we better think twice before we make our choice final. We must decide which one we choose to follow. We can't have it both ways, although many try, none-the-less you can't straddle the fence. It is one way or the other. Simple as that!

The apostles converted continually people from Judaism and from other religions so that they might serve the Lord in One Body, the Church. His Church.

This shows that God requires that every human being, regardless of where they come from, what color of their skin or what language they may speak, all be united to serve Jesus Christ and accept Him as Master in His One Kingdom, His Church because, Jesus Christ died for it.

You see, when human beings write their own religious laws, what happens is, it causes religious differences and different denominations teaching all kinds of things.

God's Kingdom teaches the same thing no matter in what part of this world you may go, the Gospel of Christ speak loud and clear, each congregation having no division of what is being taught which strictly comes from God's Word, the Bible.

Human beings are always trying to please themselves, in the old times and now, even in religious interest to suit their own purpose and desires. Instead of them singing or saying, "Have thine on way Lord," they say, "Let me have my own way Lord."

A Point of Sincere Interest

The New Testament did away with having to be stoned to death for violations committed, or sacrificing animals or even being commanded to be circumcised body wise for religious purposes. It's a good idea I suppose for parents to circumcise their male babies in this day and age but, parents aren't forced to have the procedure done. It just is not required to save your soul in serving the Lord. After all, Jesus Christ is the sacrifice and He and He alone circumcised sins.

The bottom line is we must remember Jesus Christ is our love because He first loved us. He loved us so much that He died for us. Our faith and trust is in Him and believing He is who He is, the Son of God, who is His Father and the Father of us all. This is something that should be a part of us and something we should never forget.

Chapter XII

The Early Christians

If we want blessings of Salvation and be in the family of God, we must be born again into the Lord's Church and remain faithful to Jesus Christ. The Church, Jesus Christ's Kingdom is a Spiritual Family where God has reserved a place in Heaven for His followers. This is why Jesus said, "Call no man your father (as a spiritual father) upon the earth, for one is your Father (only) which is in Heaven."

The New King James Version—Matthew 23:9 say: "Do not call anyone on earth your father; for one is your Father, He who is in Heaven.

Keep this in mind: Before anything else existed, there was Jesus Christ with God He has always been alive and is Himself God. He created ever thing, there's nothing exists that He didn't make. Eternal life is in Him.

CONCLUSION

Consider the two commandments He has given us to follow today: Matthew 22:36 40 reads: "Teacher, which is the greatest commandment in the Law?" Jesus replied: "Love the Lord your God with all your heart and with all your soul and with all your mind.' This is the first and greatest commandment. And the second is like it: 'Love your neighbor as yourself.' All the Law and the Prophets hang on these two commandments."

IN CLOSING

1 Corinthians 13:1-11, 13 reads: If I speak in the tongues of men or of angels, but do not have love, I am only a resounding gong or a clanging cymbal. If I have the gift of prophecy and can fathom all mysteries and all knowledge, and if I have a faith that can move mountains, but do not have love, I am nothing. If I give all I possess to the poor and give over my body to hardship that I may boast, but do not have love, I gain nothing.

Love is patient, love is kind. It does not envy, it does not boast, it is not proud. It does not dishonor others, it is not self-seeking, it is not easily angered, and it keeps no record of wrongs. Love does not delight in evil but rejoices with the truth. It always protects, always trusts, always hopes, always perseveres. Love never fails. And now these three remain: faith, hope and love. But the greatest of these is love. 1 Corinthians 12:12-13.

One Body, Many Parts Reminder

The body is a unit, though it is made up of many parts; and though all its parts are many, they form one body. So it is with Christ. For we were all baptized by One Spirit into One Body—whether Jews or Greeks, slave or free—and we were all given the One Spirit to drink.

First of all God tells us that we must believe in Jesus Christ, His only Begotten Son whom He placed on this earth to die for the ones who believe and trust in Him and place all their cares on Him. Then after believing in Jesus Christ sincerely, stop being ungodly, this means turning from your negative ways which are your sins, and then confess to the world that you do believe in Jesus Christ, and then be baptized for the remission of sins. Then, you have responded to the proper law, God's Law and in the proper way! And that is the true way God planned yours and my salvation. There is truly no other way, otherwise Jesus Christ leaving the comforts of His Heavenly home is of no! Use, and He died in vain.

My Prayer

I pray we remember by being born into sin and willfully being sinful, we are deserving of wrath. But because of His great love for us, God, who is merciful, has given us the chance to be alive with Christ. This is not from ourselves as some may think, or by the things we do so that we can have something to boast about. It is the gift of God. For we are God's handiwork, created in Christ Jesus to do good and be obedient to His Will which God prepared in advance for us to do.

I pray we remember that all Nationalities can be wedded with Jesus Christ by being obedient despite what others may say or what Satan and his angles deliberately put before us with worldly temptations.

I pray we remember those who call themselves "the circumcised" (which are done to the body by human hands) remember at that time they were separated from Christ without hope. But now in Christ Jesus we have a new covenant that washes away our sins by the blood of Jesus Christ. For He Himself is our peace, our Redeemer and our Savior.

I pray we remember when we are obedient to God's Will, that we are no longer foreigners and strangers, but fellow citizens with God's people and also members of His household, built on the foundation of the apostles and prophets, with Jesus Christ Himself as the chief cornerstone.

I pray we remember in Him we are joined together to become a dwelling in which God lives by His Spirit.

I pray that according to the Will of God that we repent without regret, that leads us to Salvation.

I pray that we make room in our hearts and let it be overflowing with joy knowing as we obey His Will we are pleasing our Heavenly Father.

I pray we remember that Jesus Christ has no harmony with Satan, and neither should we!

Personally, I rejoice that in everything I have brought to our attention is the truth and I have confidence in our acknowledgement of it. It is your Choice to Believe or Reject. But! Notice, When Rejecting the Truth, we are Rejecting God, not Man.

In Jesus' Name, I pray. Amen

GOD'S PART: GOD'S PLAN OF SALVATION

1. The great love of God for man, John 3:16 reads: For God so loved the world that he gave his one and only Son, that whoever believes in Him shall not perish but have eternal life.
2. He gave His Son, Jesus Christ, as the Savior., Luke 19:10 reads: For the Son of Man came to seek and to save the lost.
3. He sent the Holy Spirit as a guide. John 16:13 reads: But when he, the Spirit of truth, comes, he will guide you into all the truth. He will not speak on his own; he will speak only what he hears, and he will tell you what is yet to come.
4. He gave the Gospel as "the power" unto Salvation, Romans 1:16 reads: For I am not ashamed of the Gospel, because it is the power of God that brings Salvation to everyone who believes: first to the Jew, then to the Gentile.
5. He provided payment by the blood of Christ, Romans 5:9 reads: Since we have now been justified by His blood, how much more shall we be saved from God's wrath through Him!

MAN'S PART: OBEDIENCE

1. Hear the Gospel. Romans 10:17 reads: Consequently, Faith comes from hearing the message, and the message is heard through the word about Jesus Christ. And John 8:32 reads: Then you will know the truth, and the truth will set you free.

2. Believe the Gospel Hebrews 11:6 reads: And without Faith it is impossible to please God, because anyone who comes to Him must believe that He exists and that He rewards those who earnestly seek Him.

3. Repent of past sins. Luke 13:3 Reads: I tell you, no! But unless you repent, you too will all perish.

4. Confess Faith in Jesus Christ. Romans 10:10 reads: For it is with your heart that you believe and are justified, and it is with your mouth that you confess your Faith and are saved. And Matthew 10:32 reads. "Whoever acknowledges me before others, I will also acknowledge before my Father in Heaven.

5. Be Baptized. Galatians 3:27 reads: for all of you who were baptized into Christ have clothed yourselves with Christ. Mark 16:16 reads: Whoever believes and is baptized will be saved, but whoever does not believe will be condemned. And Acts 2:38 reads: Peter replied, "Repent and be baptized, every one of you, in the name of Jesus Christ for the forgiveness of your sins. And you will receive the gift of the Holy Spirit.

So, what does the Bible say about Salvation.

We cannot be saved by the creeds or manuals of men. In Matthew 15:9 Jesus says, "But in vain they do worship me, teaching for a doctrine the commandments of men."

Again, the Apostle Paul writes to Timothy and in 2 Timothy 3:16-17 reads: All scripture is given by inspiration of God, and is profitable for doctrine, for reproof, for correction, for instruction in righteousness: that the servant of God may be perfect, thoroughly equipped for all good works."

So then, we must look to the Word of God to learn the way of our Salvation, if we are to have hope of reaching Heaven.

So as much as in me, I have told you about the Gospel for I am like Paul, I am not ashamed to tell anyone about the free gift from God and the relationship that can be had with Him.

This is Love